Who Put All These Cucumbers in My Garden?

Who Put All These Cucumbers In My Garden?

Patricia Wilson

The Upper Room
Nashville, Tennessee

Who Put All These Cucumbers in My Garden?
Copyright © 1984 by The Upper Room
All rights reserved.

Scripture quotations not otherwise identified are from the King James Version of the Bible.

Scripture quotations designated RSV are from the Revised Standard Version of the Bible, copyrighted 1946, 1952, and © 1971 by the Division of Christian Education, National Council of the Churches of Christ in the United States of America, and are used by permission.

Scripture quotations designated TEV are from the Good News Bible, The Bible in Today's English Version, copyright by American Bible Society 1966, 1971, 1976, and are used by permission.

Book Design: Harriette Bateman
Cover Transparency: Jim Bateman / Elaine Arrowood
First Printing: February 1984 (7)
Library of Congress Catalog Card Number: 83-51398
ISBN 0-8358-0475-5
Printed in the United States of America

For
the two daisies
in my cucumber garden,

Nathan and Cherith

*Who Put All These Cucumbers
in My Garden?*

Contents

Foreword

It's a long way from daisies to cucumbers—about five years of change, growth, and more change. I've gone from being a barefooted daisy picker to being a cucumber gardener. Although that may seem to be an incongruous combination, it's actually a very compatible relationship.

As you'll read in the chapter "Spices and Cucumbers," I discovered that my life is very much like a cucumber garden: prickly, vine-covered, and full of green fruit that is sometimes indigestible and sometimes bitter. But I also discovered that from this same cucumber garden the Lord is able to produce the sweet fruits of the Spirit. It's an exciting discovery that frees me to enjoy whatever comes through my life, whether it is the mundane chore of sorting the laundry or the humbling experience of missing a deadline.

1.

Rent-a-Husband

_I have the strength to face all conditions by
the power that Christ gives me._

—Philippians 4:13 (TEV)

"Rent-a-Husband. No job too big—no job too small. I do them all," the advertisement read. *Sounds like just what I need,* I thought.

We were moving, and although both the cottage we were leaving and the one we had bought were supposedly fully furnished, there were a few things I wanted to move from one to the other. Unfortunately, it was too big a load for my car and too small a load to tempt a moving company. In short, too big for me—too small for them. But obviously, just right for "Rent-a-Husband."

I called the number. A very heavily-accented voice answered with a cautious, "Hello?"

"Is this Rent-a-Husband?" I asked, feeling a little foolish.

"Who you want?"

"Rent-a-Husband," I repeated. "Did you put an ad in the paper?"

"Yes. Yes. Is me. I put ad in paper."

"Do you do moving?"

"I move anything," the voice assured me.

"Do you have a truck?"

"How much you want to move?"

"Not too much. Just some boxes, a couple of single beds, a few bicycles, and a bureau. Oh, and a small sailboat."

15

"How big is boat?"

"About twelve feet long."

"No. No. How big? How wide?"

"Wide? About four feet, I guess. Can you do it?" I asked.

"No trouble. You see. You see. I got just the thing to do job."

His voice exuded the professional confidence I longed to hear. Feeling better every moment, I filled him in on the details. Finally, I asked the big question: "How much?"

"Not much. You see. Twenty-five dollar?"

"You've got a deal. I'll meet you Saturday morning at the old cottage at eight."

Saturday at eight I was waiting at the deserted cottage. Labor Day had come and gone and so had most of the summer residents. As I shivered in the chilly wind, I suddenly realized the position I was in. Alone in a deserted area, waiting for a man I had never met who called himself "Rent-a-Husband." I didn't even know his real name! I had just reached the stage where I had decided to go home and forget the whole thing when Rent-a-Husband arrived.

He did not drive up in a truck. He swept up the driveway in a large station wagon—about mid-1950 vintage, the kind they used to call "estate wagons." The car was more than just used and beaten up—it was a rolling, junkyard owner's dream! I forgot to worry about my safety with this Rent-a-Husband. I was too mad.

"Where's your truck?" I yelled. "That's not big enough for all this stuff."

Rent-a-Husband, who was a huge, burly man with thick dark curls and massive shoulders, shrugged and smiled depreciatingly. "You not worry, missus," he assured

16

me in his heavy accent. "This car has plenty room. You see. You see."

"But, I have a boat!"

"I know. You see. No worry." His massive hand patted my shoulder as if soothing a restless horse, and he smiled at me winningly, exposing several very large gold teeth.

Shaking off his hand, I opened the cottage door, showed him the pile inside, and stood back. Inwardly I seethed at his deception and the colossal waste of time. Now I would have to find someone else.

Rent-a-Husband merely glanced at the waiting pile. Then he went around to the open tailgate of his station wagon and pulled out a large sheet of 4′ x 8′ plywood. This he put on the roof of the car and firmly lashed it in place with bright yellow binder twine. The plywood shelved out over the hood of the car and projected another foot in the rear.

"You see," he said, pointing to the artificial shelf he had created. "Plenty room." I was not impressed.

On the plywood shelf he laid the two mattresses from the beds. On top of the mattresses went the chest of drawers, the bedsprings and frames, a rollaway cot, and a few miscellaneous boxes. Each was firmly tied with the yellow twine. The car began to sag under the load.

When Rent-a-Husband had wedged in the last box that could possibly fit on the car roof, he again went around to the open tailgate and pulled out another sheet of plywood. This he arranged to lay on the floor of the car, with about three feet hanging out past the tailgate.

"You see. You see, missus. Plenty room here."

"But there's still the boat," I reminded him through clenched teeth.

17

He answered with a flashing smile and went to get the boat, which was sitting on its small hand trailer. He adeptly rolled it up to the rear of the car. With a mighty heave, he shoved the boat into the waiting car, over the piece of plywood, bow first. It just fit from side-to-side.

"Four feet," he said. "I measure."

The stern of the boat rested on the protruding plywood at the rear. He ran some of the twine through the bow rings of the boat and out the car's open side windows. Then he lashed it to the door handles.

"Won't move now," he assured me.

I wondered if my marine insurance included Rent-a-Husband.

Into the open boat went the hand trailer, three bicycles, the sails and kit bags, and an incredible assortment of items. Finally, he lashed the mast to the door handles on the passenger side of the car.

Flashing another smile, Rent-a-Husband produced a dirty piece of red cloth from his pocket. This he tied to the boat's rudder, which was still attached to the stern. "Now we legal," he said. "You see."

Legal! Did he have any idea of what he was proposing to drive? The car was loaded beyond belief, with every possible point of vision obstructed by plywood shelves, boxes, bikes, and boats. If ever there was a disaster waiting to happen, this was it!

"Now I follow you," he said, sliding his bulk into the small space left behind the wheel.

"I'll drive slowly," I promised.

"No worry. You see. You see. I keep up easy."

"I'll stick to the back road," I suggested.

"No matter. They all know me. I no mind. You just drive like always, and I follow. You see."

18

Mentally saying good-bye to the last of our cottage possessions, I started off down the dirt road, keeping a wary eye on Rent-a-Husband in my rearview mirror. At every pothole, I waited for the whole incredible load to either slide off or out, but it didn't.

When we got to the paved road, Rent-a-Husband started to tailgate me and waved at me to speed up. Soon we were barreling down the highway at just under the speed limit.

I slowed down for the small town on the way and hoped that we could drive through inconspicuously, but Rent-a-Husband waved and honked at the gaping faces of pedestrians and drivers along the way. I began to heartily wish that the journey was over.

As we came to the final stretch of highway, Rent-a-Husband, no doubt impatient with my cautious driving, pulled out and passed me. If I had thought that he looked odd in my rearview mirror, the view of him in front of my bumper was unforgettable.

Belching clouds of black smoke, Rent-a-Husband swept down the highway. From the back of the station wagon the rudder of the boat waved gently back and forth in the breeze, its red flag fluttering like a thumbed nose to all those who doubted the moving skills of Rent-a-Husband.

O to have the sublime self-confidence of Rent-a-Husband. To be able to see beyond the limitations of my small station wagon and realize that it had limitless potential for bigger and better things! How much easier it is to say that I'm not equipped to handle a job—especially if it's something the Lord wants me to do and I don't really feel "up to it."

As a Christian, I should be like Rent-a-Husband—absolutely confident that the vehicle the Lord has given me is absolutely right for the job, no matter how unsuitable it may look to me, or to the rest of the world.

P.S. When Rent-a-Husband drove up to our new house, horn blowing, red flag waving, we made a lasting first impression on our new neighbors. They knew without a doubt that "we" had arrived!

2.

Real Estate Dealing

He leads me beside still waters;
He restores my soul.

—Psalm 23:2-3 (RSV)

"How will I know if I should buy it or not?"

"If the train's on time and the real estate agent is there to meet you, it's the right place."

It was, and he was, so I bought it—a one-hundred-acre farm complete with barn, large house, and tree-shaded drive. A gift, I thought at the time, straight from the Lord.

It all looked so good—at least in the two hours I had to inspect the property, no obvious faults were apparent. I was smart enough to realize that the pump in the wellhouse would have to be replaced, and, of course, the electricity was turned off, but a call to the hydro company would fix that.

I bought the farm on Thursday. I said good-bye to my old job on Friday and to my house on Saturday. I prepared to move the following Friday—East to a new job, new life, and now, a farm as well!

We arrived in Prescott on Friday of the July-first long weekend. It was hot—particularly after five hours in a car packed to the "gunwales" with ten potted plants (including a prickly one), two people, two cats, four fish (in a tank of water!) and one newt.

The banker who owned the farm directed me across

23

the street to the lawyer, who supposedly had everything ready to sign. The lawyer had gone for the weekend, but when his secretary saw my mother sitting in the car, a dog on her lap, a cat at her ear, and a plant between her knees, she took pity on us and gave us the keys to the farm.

"Don't worry about the official closing," she told us. "We'll get to that once you're settled in." I knew then I was made for the country.

And so we arrived! The farm had been deserted for a year and looked lonely and barren in its knee-deep cover of lawn grass. We brushed aside last year's dead leaves and unlocked the door. Home—we'd finally come home.

Our furniture was piled to the ceiling of the living room. Beds on tables, couch upside down, everything everywhere and every which way.

"Never mind that," I told my mother confidently. "Tea first, and then we'll unpack the pile." I found the stuff for tea and turned the tap. No water. For the first time, I had an inkling that there was a snake in our garden. Less confidently, I flicked the light switches. No lights, except for one dim bulb in the basement. There was hydro—but barely!

I did not, as is my usual practice, cry, fling myself about, blame a cat, or even inquire bitterly if "anybody up there was paying attention." I was too tired. I found a phone at a neighboring farm. I also found a helping hand, some buckets of water, and the name of a good plumber.

Since then, our heavenly gift has needed a new well, a new furnace, a new water pump, a new sump pump, a new electrical system, and a new set of pipes. It has not needed a new roof.

P.S. We call it Stillwater Farm for two reasons: One, from the Twenty-third Psalm—"He leads me beside still waters. He restores my soul" (which God has, most undoubtedly); and two, no matter how we try, or how much we do, there is always, somewhere, usually unexpectedly, still water dripping. Perhaps it is to remind us that even in paradise, we still need to rely on God's hand.

3.

The Cottage Water Pump

*This is the confidence which we have
in [Christ], that if we ask anything
according to his will he hears us.*

—1 John 5:14 (RSV)

For eleven months, three weeks, and six days, I think that owning a cottage is a great idea. But, on that other day of the year, I wonder who in their right mind would want one. Why? Because that's the day that we turn on the water pump.

It's a relatively simple job. Read the instructions, plug in the pump, and *voilà*—water. No problem.

No problem, that is, if you can decipher the instructions that were written for someone with a Ph.D. in pumpology and were illustrated with diagrams for the Model XK4. (Ours is the Model XK3, of course, but they assure us that there is no "basic" difference between the two.)

After five years of following the same instructions, I think I have them memorized. And I now know what the nonbasic differences between the two models are!

First of all, we must screw in the bolts that were removed when the pump was drained last fall. After the first year of the rust-removal process for the bolts, we learned to oil them when we removed them. (Oh, yes— that's one of the nonbasic differences: bolt A goes into bolt hole B on our model.)

After year two, when even well-oiled little bolts would *not* slide neatly into their respective little holes, we decided to leave the darn things in, in the fall. That took care of Instruction #1—the bolts were already in place.

Then, we must take out the big plug on the pipe where the water is poured in to prime the pump. (More about priming later.) The big plug has one little drawback—it requires a one-of-a-kind specialized monkey wrench. After year two, we had the wrench.

Even with the wrench, we can't get a good turn at the thing because the plug is neatly hidden away. After year three, we just oiled the plug down, turned it in by hand, and used the wrench for the final tightening.

We ignored the next instruction for several years. It says to take off the nose cap and rotate the shaft by half a turn counterclockwise. The instruction is accompanied by a diagram labeled "Nose Cap"; an arrow points in the general direction of the pump motor.

The reason that we ignored this instruction for several years is that we couldn't find the nose cap or anything that vaguely resembled such a thing. Anyway, the pump usually managed to start eventually, even without a rotated shaft. Until year four.

It was the Year of the Nose Cap. We pushed, picked, pulled, turned, twisted, and wrenched every part of that pump—none of which revealed a shaft that required rotating. In the end, we had to resort to the assistance of a friendly neighbor. He stopped by, took one look, flicked off the end of the pump with his screwdriver tip, and deftly turned the shaft. I promise you—only a pumpology person could have known that the little bump on the end of the pump could be popped off like a pop bottle cap. This year I personally popped off the nose cap and turned the shaft one half-turn counterclockwise.

At this point, the instructions tell us to pour some water into the pump to prime it before we can turn it on.

This assumes, of course, that even though the pump is not working, we have water available to pour into it. The amount of water needed usually runs to a bucketful or two. The next year, we remembered to bring rope so that we could lower the bucket down the well to get the water to prime the pump!

Then, plug-in time. This was, and still is, the worst moment. The pump starts up with a characteristic hum, which builds to a wallshaking crescendo. We should be able to hear the water gurgling through the pipe as the pump fills the reserve tank, reaches pressure, and turns itself off. At this writing, it has never done that.

It has pumped through hoarded buckets of priming water, and nothing else. It has run on and on until the motor has overheated. It has stopped long before any kind of pressure has built up. It has developed leaky gaskets in all the vital places. It has blown a fuse or two. Once, it didn't even hum when we plugged it in.

And so begins the day that I dread above all others at the cottage: The Day of the Pump. For the next four or five hours, we fiddle with that pump. We take it apart, put it back together, pour in buckets of icy water, clean out the foot valve in the well, check the pipes to the well, clean out the well, change the fuses, buy new gaskets, rotate the shaft, tighten the bolts, turn the taps on and off; and when all that fails, shout, cry, scream, blame the weather and water, and generally rue the day that we decided to keep the cottage for another year.

Exhausted, we stamp off to our respective rooms or disappear for a walk on the beach. And always, one of us quietly returns to the pump and prays. Finally, the pump hums and reaches pressure, and water gurgles out the tap.

Every now and then, I have a Day of the Pump in my

31

Christian life as well. Everything goes wrong—I know God isn't paying attention, and I wonder why I bother anymore.

I have all my Christian instructions memorized—be good, love your neighbor, go to church, tithe from your income, give to charity—but everything seems to be going wrong.

Usually on these days, I yell, threaten to get rid of the menagerie, refuse to eat supper, and bewail the day I ever decided to become a Christian. Then, someone prays—not always me—and "the pump hums."

P.S. When it's a lovely summer day at the cottage, the pump is far behind me, and I forget all its problems. But this year, I'm going to write *"Pray First"* on the sheet of instructions—if I remember.

4.

Looking Around the Barn

May God, the source of hope, fill you with
all joy and peace by means of your faith, . . .
so that your hope will continue to grow
by the power of the Holy Spirit.

—Romans 15:13

I love having people visit me at Stillwater Farm, and I always include a visit to the barn as the highlight of their grand tour. (I might add here that the "grand tour" is a requirement of every visitor: no tour, no lunch! After all, I didn't saddle myself with a hundred acres for nothing. I need a few "oohs" and "ahhs" to get me to the next mortgage payment.)

The barn is a very important piece of rural architecture—at least to my eyes. It is a large barn with nicely weathered grey barnboard (except where a previous owner did the east wall in alternate stripes of red and green stucco paper). Leaning picturesquely on one side, it is surrounded by businesslike paddocks and fields.

The central portion is a lofty two-stories high, and the pigeons always put on a show in the rafters for my visitors. On either side are two rings of stalls, stables, sties, sheds, and coops. Obviously, Noah could have easily started his collection in my barn.

I like to start my visitors off in the central hay mow. It's a good place to expound on the virtues of bringing in one's own hay, and with the pigeons wheeling overhead, you can almost hear the happy cries of children as they jump into the waiting stacks. If the sun is shining, the dust motes from the beams just add to the cathedral magnificence of my hay mow.

35

I allow my guests a few minutes to take it all in and then gently lead them through to the animal quarters. With quiet pride, I point out the concrete spillways in the cattle stalls and the ramped doorways to the fenced pastures outside. I lean against the hand-hewn cedar posts and talk knowledgeably about Jersey versus Hereford and the problems of choosing between dairy and beef farming. In the pigsty, I expound on the ease of raising pigs and of finding a good local butcher. I make sure the visitors appreciate the easy access to the outside wallows and the convenience of the nearby wellhouse.

In the chicken house, I extol the virtues of fresh brown eggs and explain how much better it is to have free-range chickens.

I really warm to my theme, though, in the paddock. Imagine being able to gallop freely over the fields and to hear the welcoming whinny of your favorite horse as you bring it an apple from the orchard behind the house. At this point my guests are usually speechless, overcome, no doubt, by the wonder of it all. My barn seems to have that effect on people.

I'm sure they don't see the small details—the sagging doors, the two years' deposit of manure in the cow shed, the cracked windowpanes, the moldy hay in the mow, the sunken foundations, the broken gate, or the waist-high growth of weeds surrounding the barn.

I'm sure they see the barn as I do—a symbol of hope for the future. Through the eyes of hope, the old barn becomes all I hope that it will one day be. The cows ruminate blissfully in their stalls, happy children play in the mow; and a horse enjoys an apple from an orchard yet-to-be-planted.

Sometimes, when I sit and look at the old barn of my

life—when I wallow in the details of empty hours, broken relationships, or sagging faith—I remind myself that this old barn is the hope of the goodness to come. Where the rest of the world sees an imperfect Christian, faults, failings, and all, God sees the perfect person he has planned me to be.

P.S. If my guests are really "sold" on my barn, I take them to see the pond. It's really a large mud hole, but to me it's a place for trout, small swimmers, and perhaps a duck or two. Well, why not? I can hope, can't I?

5.

Defrosting the Fridge

---

*See how patient a farmer is
as he waits for his land to
produce precious crops.*

—James 5:7 (TEV)

It all started when I decided to defrost the fridge. That in itself wasn't such a bad decision, but the timing was definitely wrong. It was already 10:00 P.M.—far too late to start a job of the proportions of my freezer's accumulation of frost. But, I had been promising my freezer that I would relieve it of its icy burden for weeks, and it was fast approaching a permanent ice age.

So I began. Of course, I soon realized that the process was going to take too long. One hour later the surface of the icebound box had merely begun to drip. Feeling very scientific and clever, I placed a pot of boiling water in the freezer section and closed the door.

After thirty minutes, the pot had frozen solidly to the bottom of the box, and the rough, icy sides of the freezer were now smooth. But, little ice had actually melted. At this point, I contemplated admitting defeat. But, having wrapped all the freezer goods in towels, I hated to have to start all over again on another day. I decided to hasten the process further.

First, I tried aiming my blow hairdryer at the icy walls. This did have an interesting effect. Although the volume of the ice did not seem to change appreciably, the ice did form lovely lace patterns and etched swirls.

After a while, my arm got tired of holding the dryer, and the steady drip of the ice water upon the electrical appliance was definitely making me nervous. Besides, although the theory was sound, the practice was not defrosting the fridge.

Now I was not only determined—I was mad. There had to be some way to remove ice from the sides of a freezer cabinet. Inwardly hating the man who had invented the darn thing just to keep *his* food cold, I searched for a weapon with which to attack the beast.

Rummaging through the junk drawer, I spotted a hammer. Wonderful! A little force should do the trick. Tentatively, I tapped the sides of the still ice-bound chest. A brief flurry of clunkings within the walls resulted. Feeling heartened by this evidence of success, I swung again. More chunks fell, missing the bottom tray of the fridge and skittering across the kitchen floor. Each tap brought a deluge of ice, falling into cold, wet puddles around my bare feet.

Then the deluge stopped, and I realized that the ice left was firmly frozen to the walls of the chest. No amount of tapping could jar it loose.

Back to the junk drawer. Aha! A small chisel. Perfect. Just what the job needed—a little leverage. Within minutes I was really getting into the swing of it. Set, tap, clunk. Set, tap clunk. I was winning at last! Set, tap, clunk. Set, tap, hiss.

Hiss? I had done it. Just as thousands of owner's manuals had warned me and as hundreds of salespeople had predicted, I had punctured one of the ribs carrying the Freon gas through the freezing unit.

The fridge continued to hiss all night, well into the next day, and long after all the frozen food had thawed and the final chunk of ice had fallen from the sides. As the poor beast breathed its last wheezing gasp of Freon, I realized that it was my impatience that had done the damage. In my hurry to remove the ice, I had forgotten the delicate core beneath.

I have done that with people, too. I have been so anxious to rush past their icy outer defenses that I have inadvertently penetrated that heart-of-hearts that we all hold most close to ourselves. And they, in fear and dismay, have run away from the smashing hammer and chisel I disguised as concern and zeal.

O Lord, when will I learn to do it your way—to let the barriers melt away naturally until the exposed heart is open and ready to receive you.

P.S. I eventually bought a frost-free refrigerator. A cop-out? Perhaps—but more likely a realization of my limitations.

6.
Time

My times are in thy hand.

—Psalm 31:15

"Can you write a short article on 'The Creative Use of Time'?" the newspaper editor asked. "You're a very busy person, but you seem to make such good use of your time."

I modestly accepted the compliment and the assignment. I do seem to make good use of my time, don't I?

I hold down a demanding full-time job, usually belong to at least one community group, am a mother (and occasionally "father") to two children, maintain a large house and property, and still find time to write, sew, paint, and watch the birds. Who better to write an article on "The Creative Use of Time"?

The deadline for the copy crept closer, but I wasn't worried. I knew that I do my best work under pressure. I could afford to wait a little longer before getting down to it. When the creative time was right, I would sit down at my desk, pull together a few succinct thoughts, and write an article worthy of a creative-time user!

Time ticked by, as it has a habit of doing, and a little nudge of worry began to gnaw at me. I had to get to it—sit down and write, soon!

The deadline began to loom over my every waking moment. In a panic, I called the editor and asked for a two-week extension. My reputation for producing on time

47

earned me a reprieve. He was willing to wait another two weeks.

"I'll make time," I told myself grimly. "After all, it won't take long. I know what I want to say. All I have to do is write it down."

Time after time I was determined to get the article done. Time after time something else came up—not necessarily more important, but more pressing, more urgent:

—the bird feeders needed replenishing, and I loved watching the nuthatches;
—Nathan wanted new jeans for school, and the stores were open until nine;
—one of my favorite old movies was on television, and I might not get another chance to see it;
—the church rummage sale would probably have just the used lawn mower I wanted; and
—the sun was shining and everyone was going for a walk in the woods.

One morning, the newspaper arrived in the mailbox. My article wasn't in it. Time had caught up with me. What a blow to my esteem. Worse still, what a blow to my reputation. I had done it—missed a deadline! So much for *my* creative use of time.

Time—that worrisome thing. It either creeps by on leaden feet or rushes through our lives like a runaway train. We've only been given so much of it to use, and when it's gone, we don't have a second chance.

Or do we? I believe that the Lord can reconcile lost moments—not in the literal sense of time travel, but in a spiritual sense. When, in my weakness I have let God's time slip through my fingers, God is able to redeem my weakness and bring good from my lost moment.

The opportunity that was there can and will come again if we ask for it: An unspoken word can be spoken, a needed touch given. And for those of us who pride ourselves in our creative use of time, the lost moment becomes a tool of humbling. We learn that we are not nearly as much in control as we like to think we are.

P.S. I think I'll buy myself one of those fancy watches that "beep beep" an alarm—just as soon as I have time to go shopping.

7.

Baking for the Bazaar

---

*If God be for us, who can be
against us?*

—Romans 8:31

The note was pinned to the bulletin board when I got home from my meeting with Nathan's teacher.

Mrs. B. called. Could you make two desserts for the bazaar on Thursday?

My heart sank. Thursday—three days and 1,745 "to-be-dones" away! Could I make two desserts? Impossible. Then I remembered Mrs. B. She was the lady who spoke to the unit meeting last year. Her subject: "A Woman's Place Is *Still* in the Home." Her thesis: A working wife and mother could not possibly run a home. By choosing to work (economic considerations aside), she was selfishly depriving her family of the life they deserved. *Did that life include making desserts for the bazaar?* I wondered. *Definitely,* I decided.

OK, Mrs. B—stand back! I am going to bake a dessert of such gastronomical and calorific beauty that they'll be standing in line until the last crumb is licked clean from the plate. I'll strike a blow for working women that will resound across the nation—well, around the block, anyway.

Fortunately, I like to cook. I am a good cook. In fact, I am an excellent cook, so the task I had set myself was well within the realm of possibility (unlike many other tasks I have rashly undertaken). The only problem facing me was the choice of delight I would prepare. I wasted precious hours perusing my multitude of cookbooks, tastebuds quivering as I contemplated "Mousseline au Chocolate" and "Vanilla Supreme a la Creme." Finally, I narrowed the field down to two tempting beauties. Which would it be? In a moment of supreme confidence, I decided to make both of them. *Two* incredibly luscious culinary masterpieces.

For once, I left myself plenty of time and started early Wednesday evening. Humming a little tune (I think it was "We Shall Overcome"), I set out to face the challenge I had set myself. Cup followed cup, measure followed measure, and surely, smoothly, the masterpieces began to take shape under my skillful hands. Everything worked the way it was supposed to: the chocolate melted smoothly, the cream didn't curdle, and the gelatin set. Already, I was savoring the triumph to come—"However do you do it, working and all . . . ?" "Oh, it's nothing really; just a matter of priorities and planning."

The final moments were fast approaching. Treat number one was happily baking in the oven. Through the window, I could see it rising to majestic heights. Treat number two was simmering gently on the stove, its golden moment of perfection nearly upon me.

I stood happily before the stove, wrapped in self-congratulations. And then—the lights went out! Frantically, I raced for the flashlight and fuse box—to no avail. The power was off in the entire neighborhood. It stayed off long enough to flatten a cake and cause a delicate sauce to set hard as a rock.

What did I do? Did I panic and try to rescue the disasters on the stove? Did I scream at the hydro company?

Did I curse the small transmitter whose failure had done this to me? No. I did the only possible thing to do under the circumstances. I cried.

And through my tears, I realized that I was not crying for the spoiled desserts. I was crying for my spoiled self-image. I had not been creating these desserts for the enjoyment of others. I was creating them for my own gratification. They were my way of telling the world that I was OK.

How futile I am in my search for OKness. Even a dessert can bolster my wavering self-image. Why does it never occur to me to allow my Creator to do the bolstering? I so easily forget that God is the one who *always* sees me as OK and doesn't require proof! Only the Mrs. B.'s of this world require proof, and who needs to impress them when the Lord of Lords and King of Kings thinks I'm OK!

P.S. Thursday after work, I ran around to the corner bakery and bought two good, but not spectacular cakes. I slipped them out of their cardboard boxes and carefully deposited them on my own plates. At the bazaar, I *didn't* say that I had made them myself, but on the other hand, I didn't say I hadn't!

55

8.

Sorting the Wash

---

*As the heart longs for flowing
streams, so longs my soul for thee,
O God.*

—Psalm 42:1

If someone were to make a list of household tasks and I were to number them in order of preference, sorting the wash and putting it away would be off the bottom of my number scale. Not that the job is arduous, or even tedious—it's not even the fact that the job is boring (same old shirts, same old jeans, same old underwear).

It's because of the socks, or the *lack* of them, or more specifically, the lack of *one* of them, that I detest the job. Regardless of the time and care I spend in carefully segregating the socks from the mishmash of the laundry, when it comes to the final stages, there's always one missing.

Because of this recurring phenomenon in my laundry room, I avidly scan the household hints columns of ladies' magazines, searching for the perfect method to keep the socks together. So far I've tried:

1. Pinning the socks together—great idea, but my household is always on the verge of a disaster that requires the remedy of an immediate pin. Frayed nerves are not helped if I say brightly, "Oh, all the safety pins are in the wash."

2. Tying the socks together—another great idea, but nobody tells you what to tie them with. I tried wool, but it shrank in the dryer, and I had to cut the darn stuff off with my nail scissors, nicking a sock in the process. I tried

string, but I couldn't undo the knots, and I had to cut the darn stuff off with . . . ditto the rest. I tried soft yarn, but the colors ran, and my son did not appreciate his new pink-and-white-striped gym socks.

3. Clipping the socks together with a clothespin—a good suggestion, until you listen to a dozen clothespins spinning around in a dryer. It's a cross between having a rifle range in your basement and having someone throwing marbles down the drainpipes. Believe me, it is not conducive to the contemplative life!

I have resigned myself to the fact that in every wash at least one sock, and more likely two socks, will be AWOL (absent without leave).

Where do they go? I have several pet theories. Here's a sampling of several of my more plausible ones:

We are being invaded by extraterrestrial life which comes to earth disguised as socks. Every once in awhile, their tour of duty on earth is up, and they are instantly recalled to their native planet.

The inner core of the earth is kept molten by a constant fuel supply of socks. This fuel is gathered by industrious little creatures who sneak through the cracks around the dryer door and steal the socks.

The socks are going to take over the world. They are marshaling their forces, one at a time, and once they have undermined our confidence with their disappearing act, they will take over and govern us by a benevolent dictatorship. The speculations are endless.

Sometimes, I feel like an odd sock, too. I feel a yearning, longing, urging that is a symptom of my "odd-sockness." My other half—my spiritual half—lives at the heart of God all the time, and as I journey toward that half, I travel through deep valleys, on untraveled roads, and onto serene mountaintops. It is this risking, exciting, questing journey that makes the Christian life so abundant!

Thank you, Lord, that you summon us to wholeness, the odd socks in the laundry of life!

P.S. I still hate sorting the wash. However, I do feel a kindred spirit with those lost socks. Who knows what adventures they are having, what wonderful nooks and crannies they have discovered? And all because they are odd!

9.

Stopped-Up Sinks

Why am I so sad?
Why am I so troubled?
I will put my hope in God,
and once again I will praise . . .
my savior and my God.

—Psalm 43:5 (TEV)

A friend gave me a little gift yesterday, which I opened when I got home from work. It was a small plaque which read:

> I love my little kitchen, Lord,
> I love each shining nook.
> The gleaming rows of pots and pans,
> Each on a little hook. . . .

I didn't get any further. Partly because I didn't want to continue on an empty stomach, and partly because I was standing in my little kitchen at the time.

My eyes slid around the room and stopped at the sink. It was not full of dirty dishes, but it was full of greasy water. Only a desultory bubble breaking the surface of orange peels and coffee grounds showed that it was still in pain. (Yes, I know that I'm not supposed to empty coffee grounds in the sink, but at 7:00 A.M., I thought I was emptying the teapot.)

So much for my little kitchen! The littered counters, one with remains of breakfast peanut butter, were bad enough, but even Mr. Clean would have run gibbering from the "nook" where I kept the cat's dish! "Gleaming pots and pans"—hah! That little ditty must have been written by a sadistic ad agency selling kitchen cleansers.

I sat and wallowed in my guilt for a while, moaning over my continuing inability to keep up with the housework. I was a washout, a never-ran, and the clogged sink was the final evidence of my worthlessness. Looking around the kitchen I thought, *How can I love anything that so closely resembles a postdisaster movie?*

Come to that, I reasoned glumly, *why would God want to love me?* My inner sink was more than just clogged—it was sealed shut. I was quite prepared to stop right there and enjoy a little self-pity, but I realized that I would need the sink before I could start supper. Resigned to the unavoidable task, I left my mournful musings to find the Drano.

The Drano finally surfaced in the broom closet where it had been lurking behind the silver cleaner. I poured a generous measure into the murky waters of the sink and waited. Moments later, the pipe rumbled ominously, and after a few tense seconds when all went very still, it heaved a mighty belch of relief. The water gurgled away, leaving behind only an eggshell or two as silent witnesses to the earlier disaster.

If only it were that easy with me, I thought. Most of the time I seem to sit in a murky state, the garbage of yesterday still floating on the surface of my life. What I need is a good dose of spiritual Drano!

Then I had one of those nasty moments when things become blindingly clear. God often tried to administer a clearing dose to me, but I valiantly resisted all his efforts. I didn't want to unclog—if I did, I might be put back into action. I liked it in my safe little world.

I looked at my sink again. I ran the tap, first cautiously and then more confidently. I watched the water swirl and eddy down the now-free drain. How like the

Spirit it is—clear and sparkling and moving! Watching the water, I realized that I wanted the Spirit to run like that through my life. Pour on the spiritual Drano, Lord. That's what I want—to be free!

P.S. I bought myself a new plaque. It reads, "Bless This Mess." Somehow, it seems to lend itself more to the decor of my kitchen. But right beside it is the gift from my friend, a constant reminder that God is always willing to help us houseclean, if we will allow it.

10.

A Clutter-Free Environment

*Do not lay up for yourselves
treasures on earth, where moth and rust
consume and where thieves break
in and steal.*

—Matthew 6:19 (RSV)

"If in doubt, throw it out" has always been one of my favorite maxims. While some people glory in a manicured lawn or a set of gleaming bathroom taps, I really like a clutter-free environment.

By "clutter-free" I don't mean a shining counter top with only three canisters or a drawer with the lingerie neatly folded into color-coordinated piles. By clutter-free, I mean free from all extraneous objects that have no possible present use. The key word here is "present."

One of my favorite Saturday morning exercises is to root through my closet and get rid of all the clothes that are out of style, don't fit, need major repairs, or have lost their appeal. My rule of thumb is if I haven't worn it in the last twelve months, out it goes. Good-bye slacks that are a size or two too small. So long dress in purple suede. See you around skirt with the broken zipper. Ditto the jacket I never really liked and the shoes that pinch my bunion.

I enjoy getting into the kitchen drawers, too. I usually bring along a big plastic garbage bag for that job. Out go the hoarded wads of string, the three thousand ties from plastic bags, the bread wrappers, the twenty-three ice-cream parlor spoons, and all the miscellaneous bags, boxes, stamps, and jar tops that someone has carefully accumulated. If I'm really in the mood, I'll move on to the kitchen cupboards and say good-bye to all the spice jars with a few grains left in the bottom and to all the cereal boxes full of crumbs.

On a really good day, I can hit the fridge as well. That's a veritable gold mine of leftovers. Usually, I need another large plastic bag by this time.

The hall closet is another favorite spot. The broken hockey stick, Cherith's one roller skate, the torn plastic rain poncho, two broken umbrellas, and someone's gold link belt—they all meet the same fate: into the garbage bag.

As my momentum builds, I head for the desk. Old bills, canceled checks and three-year-old letters—this is the real thing! I can spend hours going through the drawers, and I can still look forward to the filing cabinet.

The children cower and gibber in their rooms as they hear the approach of my footsteps and the rustle of my garbage bag. Cherith's room is particularly rewarding: she saves everything from a crumpled spelling list dated last November to the candy wrappers from her Halloween hoard.

Of course, this clearing out does meet with some protest from my family. They all claim that they need whatever item it is that I hold poised over my garbage bag. "Nonsense," I say firmly as I dump in the gym socks with no heels and three almost-empty deodorant sticks.

What they need, I tell them, is someone like me who has the intestinal fortitude to throw all the junk out. Why, if it weren't for people like me, the world would be piled high with useless stuff—stuff that someone thinks might someday be needed by someone, somewhere, for something.

Fortunately for my family, this clearing-out fever only

strikes once or twice a year. The rest of the time I spend hours looking for something that I'm sure I'd never throw out. Take that purple suede dress, for example. I know that I'd never throw that out since it exactly matches the earrings Nathan bought me for my birthday. And what happened to the cereal crumbs I was saving for a meatloaf? And why can't I ever find a piece of string in this house when I need it?

P.S. I'm glad God doesn't like a clutter-free environment. If God were to judge things by whether or not they were useful, I'm afraid my fate would be the cosmic garbage bag. I like to think that God keeps me around because he sees endless possibilities for me.

P.P.S. One other observation: have you noticed that the "If-in-doubt-throw-it-out" people always seem to live with "Put-it-away-for-another-day" people?

11.

"Comes Unassembled"

A wise man... built his house
upon the rock; and the rain fell, and the
floods came, and the winds blew and beat
upon that house, but it did not fall.

—Matthew 7:24-25 (RSV)

UTILITY GARDEN SHED. *Comes unassembled.*
All you need is a screwdriver...

"I'm going to get one," I told my mother. "All you need is a screwdriver to put it together. Even I have a screwdriver in my toolbox."

That same afternoon I drove to the local hardware store and picked up the economy model. I was a little surprised when they handed me one long, flat package about 6' x 2'. I reminded myself that all I needed was a screwdriver, and I did have that.

When I got home, I opened the package and took out the instructions. I felt a niggle of doubt when they turned out to be a lengthy tome of thirty-odd pages, but I remembered that I did have my screwdriver and I was prepared.

The first five pages told me how to build a concrete base for my garden shed. How come the advertisement never mentioned the need of a cement truck? I decided to forego the cement base.

The next five pages told me all the awful things that would happen to my shed if it weren't built on a concrete base. The section concluded with a disclaimer from any kind of warranty if the base were omitted. It still hadn't said what to do with the screwdriver.

Finally, the instructions got down to the nitty-gritty. It was good old part A into part B all over again. After years of bicycles, water pumps, and dollhouses, I am an expert at part A and part B.

At last, they mentioned the screwdriver, with a note that the job would be 99 percent more efficient and the shed 99 percent stronger if an electric drill were used. Well, I decided we'd just have to settle for no warranty, 1 percent efficiency, and 1 percent strength because a screwdriver was all I had in my toolbox.

Slowly, the bottom frame went together. Amazingly, the screw holes lined up fairly well. Another first for the wonderful world of prefab. Then it was time to put in the wall panels: 6' x 2' metal sheets. I ran into my first problem. I'm only five feet two inches, and even with my arms stretched, I could barely reach the top frame. Mother and a chair came to the rescue.

We got the panels fitted into the bottom frame and had just begun to put the top frame on when a gentle breeze blew up. The panels, unsupported on top, blew back and forth gently, twisting and groaning as they did so. Nathan and Cherith helped hold them still while I screwed the top frame into place. The screw holes weren't lining up well anymore.

The breeze swelled to a gusting wind that immediately blew the whole thing over. We lost a lot of our momentum trying to get it upright and squared off again. Several hours later, the top frame was in place. Only the roof was left to go.

The peak of the roof was eight feet high. I borrowed my neighbor's ladder. (A ladder was not mentioned in the advertisement.) Now I was using my screwdriver at an enormous height (to me), in inconvenient corners, at odd angles, and in holes that definitely didn't line up.

It took a few more hours to put the roof on, and that

included the time needed to cut back the climbing rose that grew exactly where the edge of the roof was to go. The final touch was the doors—two sliding panels that hung on special brackets. The brackets did not fit. I borrowed my neighbor's hacksaw, and they soon fit perfectly. (Add hacksaw to the list of unmentioned items.)

At this point, I ran out of screws. An hour later, I found the spare package underneath some of the packing material in the box. Dusk was coming on and so were the mosquitoes. The lintels were soon smeared with sacrificial blood.

Ten hours, 34,000 screws, and one screwdriver later, I had, as they had promised, a perfect little garden shed. It stands there, a mute monument to the wonderful never-never land of advertising. I bought it—hook, line, and sinker. I believed the "all you need is a screwdriver" line. I wanted to believe it. But in my heart of hearts, didn't I expect it would take just a little more than that? Were the cement mixer, electric drill, skilled helpers, ladders, and hacksaw really such a surprise to me? I don't think so.

I always like to think that there's an easy way to do things. Even in my Christian life, I want to believe that I can go on with a minimum of effort on my part. I hate to think that I have to do anything more than offer up a perfunctory prayer now and then. But when I come up against some of the bedrock things such as love, compassion, faith, and charity, I'm not really surprised.

Just as I was promised, with the concrete foundation of daily prayer and the power tools of the Holy Spirit, my Christian life is going to be 99 percent more efficient and 99 percent stronger. The screwdriver can do the job, but it's harder and not as rewarding.

P.S. In addition to my little garden shed, I also have one blistered palm, two strained arms, one mutilated rosebush, three disgruntled family members, and one skeptical neighbor who warns me that the whole thing will probably blow down in the first strong wind. It hasn't, but that's more due to the grace of God than to my screwdriving skill.

12.

The Birthday Treasure Hunt

*Let us run with perseverance
the race that is set before us, looking
to Jesus the pioneer and perfector of
our faith.*

—Hebrews 12:1-2 (RSV)

My two children have their birthdays on the same day. It's even more of a coincidence when you realize that they are adopted. The good Lord knew perfectly well that I was going to have enough trouble with two children without having to worry about two birthday parties as well. I've always thought that it was a nice idea of God's. Until recently.

When they were babies and then toddlers and then little folk, one birthday party was a cinch. A few balloons, two cakes (one pink, one blue), some streamers here and there, and a brisk game of pin-the-tail-on-the-donkey filled the bill nicely. The mothers usually stayed to help out and to compare notes on diaper rash and teething, or in later years, temper tantrums and neighborhood playschools.

I became quite an accomplished party giver. Until my children discovered that they were male and female. Boy and girl. Oil and water.

"I don't want any girls at my party. They just want to play with dolls."

"Do we have to invite boys? They always fight!"

I briefly toyed with the idea of two parties on two consecutive days. I toyed with it just long enough to figure out: (a) the monetary cost, and (b) the wear and tear factor on me.

"One party," I told them firmly. "Two friends each. I'll take care of the games."

"Games!" snorted Nathan. "Sissy games like pin-the-tail-on-the-donkey?"

"Games!" cried Cherith. "Can I tell Loretta to bring her Barbie dolls?"

This was proving to be more difficult than I had anticipated. After long hours of poring over "Hundreds of Things for Your Child to Do" books and reading "Creative Parties for Creative Children" articles, I was no closer to a solution than before. The only way out seemed to be to have lunch at McDonald's and then to go bowling. But my car only held four, and I dreaded the thought of driving six incompatible children down twenty miles of four-lane highway in a borrowed car.

Then my mother suggested a treasure hunt. A real treasure hunt, ranging over our hundred acres of land, with rhyming clues, hidden treats, and a buried treasure. "If they start out at 3:30," she said, "it will take them an hour or more to find the treasure, and by then it will be time to open the presents, eat the hot dogs, cut the cake, and say so long. You can send them back home at 6:30, and you'll only have had them for one 'actual' hour."

I thanked the Lord for giving me such a wonderful mother.

The children were naturally skeptical, but fortunately, they didn't have any treasure hunt experience to back up their protests.

The morning of the big day, I locked them in the house and set off to put out the clues, hide the treats, and bury the treasure. Mother and I had spent the evening before making up such deathless rhymes as:

84

Where the cows like to sleep,
You will find the next clue sheet.

We had planned twenty clues, and it took me over
an hour of hard slogging to work my way around the
course. I ignored the steady drizzle, telling myself it would
clear up by afternoon. Finally, I buried the treasure (a
toffee tin filled with "gold" coins) and headed home. I was
wet through and beat besides. "It will probably take them
a good two hours," I told Mother confidently.

When the guests arrived, each (thank heaven!) wear-
ing the boots I had instructed them to bring, I carefully
went over the rules of the hunt. "Wait for each other.
Don't run ahead. Share the clues. Watch for special
treats." I handed them the first clue, and they were off.

In what seemed like seconds they were at the barn,
over the fence, across the field, in the cedar woods. I lost
sight of them briefly, but moments later they were across
the second field; they ran full tilt up to the apple tree.
This wasn't going as I had planned.

They disappeared into the willow bush around the
pond, and I breathed easier. This part would slow them
down. But within minutes, they were back in view,
heading at high speed down the cart track. Pausing just
long enough to sweep up the next clue, they crossed the
stream, jumped the fence, and ran pell-mell across the last
field. In thirty-one minutes flat, they had reached the
buried treasure, dug it up, and shared it.

It was raining—hard. I had two and a half hours left
with six soggy children. It was a very long afternoon,
punctuated by cries of "What do we do now?" and
"Nathan keeps hitting me" and "When do we eat?" The

steady drone of the clothes dryer made a contrapuntal background to the sound of rock music from the local radio station.

When I talked to Nathan and Cherith about the treasure hunt afterwards, I discovered that they had missed a lot of the pleasures I had planned. In their haste, some of the children never even saw the clue sheet since the first one there had grabbed it, read it, and sped away. The rest had merely raced after that child. They also missed the little treats I had hidden for them along the way. At one point, in their determination to be first at the treasure, they had bypassed two fun clues altogether. Although they succeeded in finding the treasure, they missed out on a lot of the fun—sharing a clue, anticipating the next one, finding a hidden treat.

I'm the same way, too. When I set myself a goal, I head for it determinedly. If the Lord wants to take me on a side road or byway, it takes more than a mere clue to turn me aside. If there's a hidden treat for me, I'm not interested—I don't have time to stop and look around. Often, I blindly follow the people in front, thinking that they look as if they know where they are going—perhaps they have already read the clue sheet. I certainly don't take time to think about any clues I might find. I'm on the move, eager to get on with the race. I don't have time to share the clue with anyone else either. They can follow me if they want to.

I miss a lot of fun in the Christian life. I forget that to run the race with perseverance is not to run it with blinders on. When I find myself heading blindly down a course I have set for myself, I need to remember the birthday treasure hunt. I need to look for the clues, savor the hidden treats, and expect to find the treasure in a totally unexpected place. I need to reassure myself that this treasure will be infinitely more valuable and more satisfying than my original expectations.

P.S. At 6:15, I bundled all six children into my four-passenger car and drove them home personally. At 6:45, I was surveying the wreckage of the living room, wondering whose wet socks were on the coffee table and where the extra running shoe had come from.

"That was the best birthday ever," Cherith said.

"We all had a lot of fun," Nathan assured me.

Easy for you to say, kid. Easy for you.

13.

Underststudy for Noah

Ask the beasts,
and they will teach you.

—Job 12:7 (RSV)

We are one of those strange families that believes the animals should be included in every outing. Since I am fond of pointing out that our menagerie consists of two kids, two dogs, two cats, three fish, and one newt, our friends are always surprised (whether pleasantly or not depends on their penchant for animals) by what arrives with us on their doorstep.

For years we traveled back and forth to the cottage nearly every weekend and took both cats and both dogs with us. Since my standard passenger complement is my mother, my two children, and me, the animals are the icing on the cake, so to speak.

We have it worked out to a fine art. Mother and I in front. One large dog at her feet; one small dog at her side. Two children in back. Two cats in their respective cages in the luggage compartment of the hatchback.

We don't attract too much attention from passing motorists, although tailgaters have an unpleasant moment when they meet the fixed stares of the two cats looking out the back window.

It's when we stop for gas that we cause a stir. Invariably, the person pumping gas does a double take while unscrewing the gas cap and looking directly into two pairs of yellow eyes. No sooner recovered from that shock, the attendant meets a small wet nose while cleaning the front windshield. Then, when the bewildered individual comes to my window to collect the money, the large dog usually stands up and barks loudly.

At this point the attendant notices the two children in the backseat. "Holy cow," commented one service station employee. "Are you filling in for Noah or something?"

On shorter jaunts we leave the cats at home. For instance, if we're off to a local auction, we pack both kids and dogs in the car and head out. The only problem is finding a shady tree under which to park the car so that the dogs are comfortable. The house with the shady tree in front usually has a large dog tied up on the porch. The moment we leave the car, the auction sale is punctuated by howls, woofs, barks, and yelps as the incumbent dog tries to establish ownership, and our two challenge its rights.

The culmination of my pet-moving career came when we took the whole menagerie three hundred miles to our new home. I let the movers take all the furniture and agreed that I would move the most delicate of the house plants, the cats, the dogs, the fish tank, and the newt.

After long consultations with several pet shops, I found out that I couldn't move the fish tank under any circumstances. The tank would crack; the water would go stale; the fish would die of trauma. I tried to find someone who wanted an instant source of amusement and pleasure, but none of my friends were interested in one fat black molly, two carp, and a newt.

So, on the morning of the move, I loaded the car in our usual manner (minus the kids who were at camp) and drained most of the water out of the fish tank. I placed the newt in its smaller tank inside the now nearly-empty fish tank, covered the whole works with plastic, taped it down tightly so that the remaining water wouldn't slop out, and wedged the tank within a tank between the two cat cages.

For three hundred miles, neither cat moved once. They were too busy watching three fish and a newt swim by inches from their noses.

A year later, the same three fish are still enjoying their life of luxury and ease. I'm sorry to say that the newt went on to a happier land—whether the shock of two cats just inches from its nose was too much for it, I can't say.

The animals are such an integral part of our lives, it just seems natural for us to include them in our outside activities. Why shouldn't they come along to the feed store, supermarket, or auction sale?

Actually, it's similar to bringing my Christianity with me wherever I go. But, so many times, I find myself in a situation—an office party, a PTA meeting, a political rally—where I think it's inappropriate to express my Christian beliefs. I've been conditioned to think that Christianity is out of place anywhere except in church or in prayer meetings.

If my Christian life is integral to me, wouldn't it just naturally go with me everywhere? Ah—there's the cutting edge. Just how integral is it? Maybe I should be as free with my Christianity as I am with my pets. I don't apologize when I bring them along. Surely, I can give my Savior the same courtesy.

P.S. We now have twenty chickens in our menagerie. Nathan is very fond of one he calls "Friend." I'm hoping he won't decide that Friend should join us the next time we head out. But if he does, I wonder if Friend would like her very own cat cage?

14.

Christmas Shopping

---

*Every good gift and every perfect
present comes from heaven;
it comes... from God.*

—James 1:17 (TEV)

There is one aspect of Christmas that I really hate to face. It's a part of the office scene which I wish I could escape. It's nerve-wracking, traumatic, and sometimes even dangerous. No, it's not what you're thinking—I don't mind the office Christmas party. It's something else altogether.

The dreaded moment comes when someone passes the hat. If it were a hat for a charitable donation, a collection for the secretary's new baby, or even for tickets on the hockey pool, I could face them equally without a qualm.

But this is the hat that contains a number of carefully folded slips of paper. I know what they are—I put one in myself. Each paper has a name on it, and one of those names will be mine.

It's the annual method for choosing a Christmas gift recipient. Somewhere, lost in the mists of time, there must have been a moment when someone, whose name is now mercifully forgotten, decided that this would be the best way to regulate interoffice Christmas giving.

The theory behind the method is fine: one gift to buy instead of ten; one small amount of money to spend instead of a small fortune; and the assurance that even if everyone in the office hates you, you will at least receive one gift at Christmas.

In practice it's a different matter. One gift, yes, but for a person whose tastes are completely unknown to you; one small amount, fine, but it's difficult to buy a meaningful, funny, amusing, or even thoughtful gift for under five dollars; one gift at least for everyone, absolutely, if you've always wanted an embroidered typewriter cozy.

No wonder my hands tend to tremble as I dip into the hat. I can honestly say that I've never been disappointed in my slip of paper—it's always the last person I'd expect to buy anything for. The person is either on a diet or suffering from a nervous stomach—no easy way out with a box of chocolates here. Or, the individual is on the top of the office heap, with a yearly salary figure that would nicely pay off my mortgage—forget the cute little recipeholder made out of a paper cup and a plastic spoon that I picked up at the church bazaar last week. Or, the person is the most reticent I've ever met, who, as far as I know, has no hobbies, no family, no interests, no inclinations, no secret yearnings, and no hidden dreams; this employee never takes a vacation. That lets out a craft kit, travel book, steering-wheel cover, or jigsaw puzzle. You can see my problem.

In the weeks before Christmas when everyone else is cheerfully shopping for family and friends, I wander from store to store, choosing, changing my mind, and choosing again.

What to buy? What to buy? Not too flashy, but not too dull either. Cute is dangerous—I've learned the hard way that what I may think is cute may look tacky to someone else. Religious can be touchy—a gift that preaches doesn't always present the message I had in mind.

98

This year I've found a solution to the problem. I've finally thought of a gift that I can give to anyone. An angel. That's right, an angel.

Who can find fault with angels? They're Christmas, but they're not high-pressure. They're universal, but they're not unique to any one event. They represent love, caring, joy, and peace on earth—precisely what this Christmas business is all about.

I'll tell the lucky slip of paper that I draw that this little angel is a guardian angel—one who will be glad to occupy a corner of the desk or bedside table or mantelpiece, as a reminder that God watches over us all with loving care. The angel will be all that I want a gift to be— meaningful, a measure of what I think of someone, and a reminder of the meaning behind the gift.

Well, this year I'll try it and see. Actually, I'm rather looking forward to the hat now. I wonder how my executive boss will like an angel, or the crabby typist next door, or the old fellow that delivers the mail? It certainly does have possibilities—it certainly does!

P.S. There is one other small problem attached to this exchange of gifts in the office. If the gift is supposed to be some measure of what the giver thinks of me, how come last year I received a bottle of perfume called "Last Chance"?

15.

The Family Room

The wind blows where it wills,
and you hear the sound of it,
but you do not know whence it comes
or whither it goes; so it is with
every one who is born of the Spirit.

—John 3:8 (RSV)

It is cold, and it has been cold for the past week. I've already been through the car-won't-start-driveway-needs-shoveling-who-wants-to-get-out-of-a-warm-bed syndrome. And still the cold remains! Surely, if God had meant for me to get out in these chilly predawn minutes and stand in the freezing wind to wait for a long overdue bus, I would have been provided with thermal underskin. As far as I'm concerned, hell won't be fire and brimstone; it will be snow and freezing rain.

Actually, I am beginning to suspect that hell will be something like my back room. My back room (euphemistically called a "family room" by real estate agents) started its life as the coldest back shed in the nation. Haphazardly attached to the kitchen wall and optimistically fitted with windows and a door, it provided an instant walk-in freezer and the only way to get to the basement of the house. For the one who does the laundry, the walk to my basement laundromat could make a trek across Siberia seem like a summer stroll.

During a mild spell last winter, I decided to have the shed renovated, insulated, and converted into a usable room. At the same time, I would have a new basement entrance built in a more convenient location. And so, in the twinkling of a bank loan, it was done.

103

In the waning months of winter we moved the family into its room. By removing the kitchen window and door, we now had a visually-pleasing and architecturally-interesting kitchen/family room combination.

The cold returned for a few brief days in March. So did the freezer conditions of the back shed (er . . . room). Well, we told ourselves, it's just a few minor cracks and gaps to fill in. Out came the weather-stripping and caulking gun. Before we could find out whether our efforts were successful, it was spring and then summer. The family room became a cool retreat from the heat of a hot July day.

But the seasons have gone full cycle, and we are now living in the winter of our discontent in the back room. The first hint of trouble came on a blustery day of freezing rain in December. Sitting in front of the television with my family gathered around, I could hear a noise, somewhat like a mouse rustling, and every now and then feel a cold mist on my cheek.

I made several furtive forays around the room trying to locate the source of the noise. (Furtive because my mother does not care for mice and would rather sleep in a snowdrift than share her room with one of the furry rodents.) I finally tracked the sound to the children's toy boxes stacked on the old house wall under what used to be the kitchen window. But, I couldn't find any source of the sound.

Baffled, I returned to my chair. As I sat there, a movement caught the corner of my eye. The plants that now hung in the empty kitchen window frame were swaying gently to and fro. Intrigued, I pulled a chair over to the wall and climbed up. An icy blast of cold mist hit my face. The small icy particles fell to the floor below and scattered across the plastic toy boxes—I had found the "mouse."

Through the crack where the addition joined the main house, a steady stream of snow-laden air blew down across the plants, causing them to sway gently in the breeze. A small drift of snow had gathered in the corners along the old windowsill.

Out came the caulking gun. The enemy had been sighted, the battle lines were drawn, and the war was on. From that moment on, the skirmishes and minor victories were all on my side. Crack after crack fell beneath the relentless onslaught of weather stripping and caulk.

But the enemy never let up. As soon as one baseboard was sealed, another gaped. The cry of the family changed from "I want to watch Channel 7" to "I feel a draft over here!" By Christmas time, it seemed that the battle had finally been won. The back room was cool, but with the aid of extra sweaters for everyone and a quartz heater, the problem was easily overcome.

Then came the cold snap of January. In other homes pipes froze, windows cracked, furnaces gave out, and electric blankets overloaded. Not so in ours. The back room dealt the final, telling blow. The frame of the door heaved in the abnormally deep ground frost. It was a wrenching, twisting heave that meant that the outside storm door had an inch of open space at the top, and the inside door had an inch of space at the bottom. Both doors now had only two positions: stuck shut and wide open. In either position, the back room was subject to the coldest, meanest, cruelest draft that ever blew.

We fought back valiantly. In the end, the doors could be opened, although it was not a job to tackle in a weak moment. Only the bathroom habits of two dogs and two cats could induce us to attempt the feat. But despite a veritable barricade of pillows, quilts, rugs, and the odd bag of laundry, the draft crept in.

The other evening as I sat huddled in two sweaters, I felt the inevitable draft play around my well-socked ankles. And suddenly, I thought of the drafts of the Holy Spirit that blow in our lives. Sometimes they are cold and uncomfortable, signaling changes and movements that we would rather ignore. Quickly, lest they disturb the neat little boxes we have made for ourselves, we seal all the cracks and claim we never felt them blow.

When we do this, it often takes a frame-wrenching incident before we will allow them to blow through our little boxes. And once the fresh winds of the Spirit are recognized in our lives, things happen: we change, others change, and clouds of despair and doubt are blown away.

P.S. The battle is over. We moved the television into the living room, built a huge fire in the fireplace, and tried to forget that we had a family room. Come summer, we'll move back in. I wonder if I can convince the bank to agree to "seasonal payments"?

16.

Ducks in January

---

*You were like sheep that had lost their way,
now you have been brought back to follow the Shepherd
and Keeper of your souls.*

—1 Peter 2:25 (TEV)

On New Year's Day this year, in a fit of "let's-get-out-of-the-house-before-someone-goes-berserk-with-cabin-fever," we decided to go to feed the ducks. We gathered up all the leftover bread crusts in the house, bundled up for a winter excursion, and headed for the park.

I don't know why there are always ducks in the park. It seems silly to me—if I had a nice house in the sunny south to fly to, I'm sure that I wouldn't spend my winters in a lakeside park in Toronto. However, this particular flock has opted for the civilized comforts of store-bought bread in a cold climate in exchange for the feeding rat race under the southern sun. Since this was the coldest winter in recent history, I'm sure a lot of ducks regretted their decision to stay.

We arrived about midafternoon. It was bitingly cold. The lake and river mouth were frozen solid, and the ducks were huddled in shivering groups, trying to get out of the wind that blew relentlessly out of the north. The park was deserted.

I suspect that the ducks' "gravy train" had stopped as soon as the cold weather set in. They were certainly glad to see us and our small supply of stale bread. In moments, we were surrounded by the hungry hordes. Even the dogs, straining at their leashes, didn't deter the ducks that quacked and squabbled over every scrap and clustered around our legs, looking for more. Nathan was delighted when a large Canada goose waddled up and took the food from his outstretched hand.

We enjoyed it so much we decided to make it a Sunday event. Throughout January, the weather stayed cold. We became welcome visitors at the park, and the ducks greeted us with excited cries that we liked to think meant they recognized us now. They became quite adroit at dodging the lunging jaws of the leashed dogs in order to peck a dropped crumb at our feet. Nathan continued to hand-feed his favorites.

As the weather gradually warmed up, more and more people would be in the park. The ducks no longer needed us—there was plenty of bread around. They didn't care for the dogs either; they made it quite clear that if we wanted to feed our feathered friends, the dogs would have to wait in the car. Hand-feeding was a thing of the past. The ducks simply sat in midstream and waited for the food to be thrown to them.

Eventually, Sunday in the park was crowded. The litter bins were full of half-empty bread bags, and the ducks hardly bothered to reach out for the food floating past their beaks. The last time we were in the park, we left early with half a bag of bread still in our pockets. We haven't been back since. Somehow, it's no fun when you're not really needed.

I wonder if God feels that way, too. We're only too glad to be fed when the going is rough—we'll even come to shore to feed from God's hand. But in the halcyon days of prosperity and plenty, we've got lots more sources to draw on. Sometimes God's bread is lost among the crumbs of this world. Then it takes a cold winter before we really appreciate God's bounty.

P.S. We decided to go to the zoo at High Park instead. Have you ever taken a full-blooded hound dog to a zoo full of elk, deer, and raccoon? I think we'll try roller skating next week.

17.

Woodpiles

Set your affection on things above,
not on things on the earth.

—Colossians 3:2

My mother covets woodpiles. I think it must be all right since woodpiles are not listed under specific no-no's in the commandments.

However, it does make driving difficult. Every interesting woodpile elicits a comment:

"Look over there. There must be ten cords in that pile."

"What a beautiful stack. Wonder where he got the maple from?"

"There's a pile all ready for next winter."

The whole family is becoming expert at assessing woodpiles. Shapes, sizes, stackings, and cordages—all are eagerly discussed whenever a particularly promising pile is sighted.

I have nothing against coveting, mind you. I personally have felt that particular twinge over such mundane items as my neighbor's dog-free lawn or the new car in the driveway. But they pale in comparison to my mother's fixation with woodpiles.

Mother has always harbored an abiding commitment to getting in wood for the fire. When we owned a cottage, she considered it mandatory for everyone, family and visitor alike, to pick up at least two sticks for the fire on every walk. It became second nature for us to pick up every spare bit of driftwood, deadfall, or brush that we passed. Eventually I reached the stage where I would automatically pull over to the side of the road if a promising piece of wood were lying there. We were very proud of the fact that we never had to buy a bit of wood for the cottage fireplace.

When we moved to the city, one of the most important items I negotiated into the offer-to-purchase was the five cords of wood stacked in the back shed. In the depths of the coldest winter on record, I looked forward to toasting my toes in front of the fire when I got in from work. We sold the house just in time. The woodpile was down to its last few sticks.

The farm we bought met our most important requirements: a fireplace and a large woodlot. One of the first things we did was to hire two local lads to cut us some wood from our back bush. We estimated that five cords would see us through the winter to come. The wood piled up quickly outside the back door, and it looked mighty comforting when I drove up the driveway at night.

It rained in August, September, and October. The wood did not season as expected. It just lay there, soaking up the rain. In November, the whole pile froze solid and stayed that way.

Not to be daunted, Mother burned it anyway. The wood hissed and smoked and spluttered on the hearth. We longed for a good, old-fashioned, roaring fire.

Finally, we came to the end of the five miserable cords, and breathing a sigh of relief, we ordered some wood. It was wonderful stuff; dry and easily split, it crackled on the hearth and threw off a fabulous heat. It was also very expensive. As we watched it burn and calculated the cost, we remembered the acres of woodlot in the back forty. So near, yet so far!

That's where Mother's coveting really began. To have wood, wonderful wood, piles of it, stacked, split, dry, and ready, was only part of it. To have wood, free and clear, from one's own backyard—that was the heart of the matter.

And then I talked to one of our neighbors with his own woodpile. "How I envy you," his wife said. "I wish we could afford to buy some wood now and then. Our woodpile didn't season this year, and we've had to make do with the rotten old stuff. After all our work last spring, too. That sure is a nice pile of wood you ordered. Must make all the difference." They were coveting our woodpile!

It's all a giant conspiracy, a Machiavellian plan worthy of "Old Dirty-face" himself: I covet yours, and you covet his, and he covets mine! What a wonderful way to keep Christians tied up.

Instead of being thankful that we could buy wood, we were angry that we couldn't have our own wood. And it's the same way with many other things in life—it's easier to envy another's possessions or faith or personality than it is to be thankful for our own.

P.S. I think we've found the solution—whenever we pass a woodpile now, my daughter yells: "Quick! Cover up Granny's eyes!" Crude perhaps, but effective.

18.

The New Snowblower

Jesus said,
"My grace is sufficient for you,
for my power is made
perfect in weakness."

—2 Corinthians 12:9 (RSV)

Today is the first day of spring. It's my first spring here on Stillwater Farm, and I had expected to greet it with a long sigh of relief that the vicious eastern Ontario winter was finally on its way out.

After all, everyone I met last fall was more than anxious to tell me his or her winter horror tale. "You think it's bad in the North," they'd say, shaking their heads wisely. "That's nothing compared to winter here in eastern Ontario." Or, "Snow? You think that three feet is a lot of snow? Why, that's just a ground covering here in the East." Or, "I had a neighbor who was snowed in for a week . . . couldn't even get his plow to his side road. They had to bring him emergency supplies by snowmobile."

Needless to say, I was a little apprehensive about the winter to come, especially since I had chosen to live in a rural area—in the summer described as "delightfully secluded." But, I began to suspect it would be "completely isolated" from a winter point of view.

I decided to prepare for the battle ahead. First, I sold my car—a "city car" whose tractionless rear end had never had to cope with anything more than the dusting of snow left on the streets after the snowplow went by.

I seriously toyed with the idea of a four-wheel-drive vehicle. I rather liked the picture of myself in a jeep, but economic considerations aside, I realized that a jeep was not the vehicle for my sixty-mile-round-trip, daily drive to work. Besides, there wasn't really enough room for all of us—the kids, my mother, the dogs, and the cats.

In the end, I bought a small car (easier to push out of snowbanks) with front-wheel drive and a reputation for cold-weather starting. Then I prepared the car: a block heater, snow tires, heavy-duty windshield wipers, emergency pack in the trunk (blanket, food, gas, and water), a small snow shovel, and a box of unused kitty litter for those icy patches.

Now the house. I had a new furnace installed, the oil tank filled, and the chimney cleaned. I ordered a few cords of wood, just in case. We bought two radiant heaters for those inevitable cold spots, put up heavy drapes on the living room windows, and caulked all the windows.

Only one thing was left. The driveway. I admit it isn't a very long driveway, and I could probably leave my car at the end and walk to the house if I came home after a day of snow. But what about those mornings-after-the-night-before snowstorm when snow on the driveway was six feet deep and I had to get to work?

I debated whether to arrange for someone to come and plow us out, but I discovered that most of my neighbors don't get up and out to work as I do. They just mosey over to the barn and leave the driveway until another day.

The driveway was all ours—or more accurately, all mine! The time had come to investigate snowblowers. In mid-November, the first snow (a mere inch or so) jolted me into action. After a long conferral with the snowblower representative, we decided that a power-driven blower, rather than the tractor/plough setup I had pictured, would be the best way for me to go.

The New Snowblower

It didn't take much to convince me that the top-of-the-line machine was right for me. No small-time, Mickey Mouse equipment for my driveway—this was a job that called for "Super blower"! I bought the biggest, brightest, toughest, and most expensive snowblower on the lot. Even the kid who delivered it to the farm looked suitably impressed when I told him I would be operating it myself.

It turned out to be a cinch to operate, so I taught Nathan how to drive the thing and assigned him the job of Chief Snow Clearance Officer.

November wore on into December, and the fields around the farm continued to wear a dun brown coat. Nathan and I waited anxiously for our first "real" snowstorm. We wanted to see what our snowblower could do.

Christmas Eve was foggy and wet. The fog rolled in through Christmas week, and the skates and skis remained in the closet. The snowblower remained in the driveway.

In January, we told ourselves that "this was it." A light snow fell one day—thin and powdery as it blew across the lawn. Nathan tried "blowing" it, too. He blew more gravel off the driveway than anything else.

By February, we were feeling a little desperate. Every evening as I drove in on my snow tires, heavy-duty windshield wipers sluicing the rain off the windshield, I could see our snowblower, ready for action.

Today is the first day of spring. Nathan and I have yet to see action with our snowblower. As I sit in my room, watching the sleet lay a thick film of ice on the blower, I realize that this could be the story of my life. I like to think that I can anticipate the storms ahead. All I need is a little preparation time, and I can handle anything. But it doesn't work out that way. Only the Lord knows what storms I must face, and the Lord prefers to make the preparations. My little efforts are futile by comparison. They only serve to give me a false sense of security. In the end, the storm always comes from a different direction, and I am totally unprepared. "Trust in the Lord" becomes more than a nice saying.

Wouldn't it be wonderful to be the kind of Christian who really "takes no thought for the morrow"—for the storms thereof?

P.S. Remember I mentioned the sleet? That's been this winter here in eastern Ontario—sleet, hail, and freezing rain. Guess who didn't have a bag of salt ready on the back porch?

19.

June Thoughts

*For everything there is a
season, and a time for every matter
under heaven.*

—Ecclesiastes 3:1 (RSV)

Every year June bursts in on me like an excited child. Suddenly, everything has to be done *now*!

Nathan's Cub camp is next weekend—they sent home a list, but where do I find three pairs of fleece-lined socks in June?

And speaking of fleece-lined, has anyone seen the sleeping bags? Not the old ones—I know where they are. One is still draped across the cellar window, and the other is being used as a tent in Nathan's room. But where are the new ones I bought for camp last year?

Cherith tells me that she has promised Mrs. Richardson that we will take care of the school rabbits over the summer vacation. Fat chance, Mrs. Richardson. I know what happens when you leave two rabbits together over the summer vacation.

I don't know what kind of vacation we're going to have this year. I've already had two definite hints that friends would love to drop in and stay for a few days. If only they'd give a little notice—even a few hours. Then, if nothing else, I could at least clean the bathtub.

I must remember to take my winter coat to the cleaners. I guess it's safe now; we haven't had snow for three weeks. Speaking of snow, I'd better get the snowblower bedded down for its summer vacation. I'm sure there was a book of instructions with it that said something about draining this and that and unscrewing the something-or-other. I wonder where I put that book? With my luck, it's probably hiding out with the new sleeping bags.

Oh, well, I'll look for them all tomorrow. I might drop by the library, too. I want to get some new gardening books. And pick up some bedding plants at the nursery. I think I'll put in some strawberries this year. I'm sure I saw a terrific recipe for freezer jam in that magazine I was reading yesterday. Wonder where I put it?

The freezer! If I plan to fill it with more than just on-sale, day-old bread, I'd better clean it out and sort through the leftover bits and pieces from our winter's supplies. Maybe I should call the butcher and order some more beef; I'm sure there's only a package or two of hamburger left.

I'll call the butcher tomorrow. And I'll call about an appointment for Nathan's camp medical. I'd better take him shopping for some new shorts and t-shirts as well. It's unbelievable how much a ten-year-old can grow in one short year.

Actually, it's pretty unbelievable how much an adult can grow in one short year, although in my case I'm speaking of horizontal (as in side-to-side) growth. Time to start dieting again. I'll pick up some grapefruit tomorrow.

Now that I think about it, I'm sure that I put the new sleeping bags away with the summer clothes. That shouldn't be too hard to track down. I'll look tomorrow.

Maybe I should take my car in for servicing tomorrow. It's been making funny noises for a week or two now. I'll take Cherith's bike with me. I'm darned if I can fix the chain. Perhaps if I smile desperately, Mike will look at it for me. Why didn't she tell me that it was broken last month, instead of two days before the bike-a-thon?

The lawn needs cutting again. Funny how it needs cutting twenty-three times during the busiest month of the year and then stops growing when you finally have time to take care of it properly. I wonder how much grass two rabbits could eat? I'll get Nathan to cut it tomorrow.

Cherith informed me that she volunteered my services to bake decorated cupcakes for twenty-four children. The school is having a field day on Friday, and the mothers are supplying the goodies. Thanks, Cherith. Cupcakes decorated for twenty-four are just what I like to do best. I'll buy a cake mix tomorrow. Or, dare I even contemplate it, I'll stop by the bakery and see what kind of decorated cupcakes they have to offer.

Tomorrow. It seems as though I have an awful lot of things to do tomorrow. Not today. Today it's June, and the warm June sunshine is flooding my kitchen. The siren call of the first June breeze is wafting through the window.

I'm convinced that the Lord made perfect June days like this just to stop us in our tracks—to remind us that we weren't created to run around in mindless circles, doing, fixing, making, and going. We were created to smell the lilacs, feel the warm sun in our faces, and listen to the robins sing. On a perfect June day, no one can ignore the sight of a blue June sky or turn away from an inviting patch of clover.

Our Lord knows how much we need to take the time to enjoy what was made for us. But only God has the power to make creation irresistibly tempting.

P.S. I'm going to put on my too-tight shorts, spread

the old sleeping bag on the uncut lawn, and turn my back on the unserviced car, the broken bicycle, the disordered freezer, and the nonsummerized snowblower. I'm going to lie here and think June thoughts and nothing else. If all goes according to plan, I'll get my first official sunburn of the summer.

20.

Pick a Name—Any Name!

*There is salvation in no
one else, for there is no other
name under heaven given among [us] by
which we must be saved.*

Acts 4:12 (RSV)

My name is becoming a real nuisance. Ever since I reached the point in my career where I merited a business card, the problem of what to call myself has become an increasingly thorny one.

When I was married, the question resolved itself into three choices: (1) Mrs. My-Husband's-First-Name and My-Husband's-Last-Name; (2) Mrs. My-First-Name and My-Husband's-Last-Name; and (3) leave the Mrs. off and just go by My-First-Name and My-Husband's-Last-Name.

However if I went with choice number one, someone would think I was one of those poor unemancipated women who lives in her husband's shadow. That wasn't the image I wanted to project to business associates. If I went with choice number two, those who knew their etiquette would assume that I was a widow, and those who didn't might think I was ashamed of my husband's name. Choice number three was definitely risky: I might be labeled women's liberation (radical) or dominant female (dangerous).

Then, should I go by my full first name (Patricia), or full name and initial (Patricia F.), or be very informal (Pat), or try full name and familiar name together (Patricia [Pat] F.)? And then, I had to remember that Pat on its own could connote either male or female. Did I want to risk having my mail addressed to Mr. Pat . . . ? The combinations and permutations were endless.

Before I really came to grips with this dilemma, I found myself divorced and into a whole new ball game of naming. I decided to make things a little easier by resuming my maiden name. Then I didn't have to worry about being Mrs. His-Last-Name when there was another Mrs. His-Last-Name in the picture.

However, I soon discovered that there were all kinds of hidden pitfalls in the form of salutation that I chose to use in my divorced state. If I chose to call myself Miss, the look that the children's teacher gave me was definitely speculative. So was that of their Brownie leader, dentist, and Sunday school teacher. Obviously, in motherhood matters, Mrs. was the only way to go. But calling myself Mrs. was very strange. Coupled with My-Own-Last-Name, I sounded like my mother!

I felt a little fraudulent when I tried Miss. After all, I had been married, was a mother, and didn't put down spinster on my income tax form.

That left Ms. If ever there were a form of saluation that conjures up negative response, it is Ms. Male business associates presumed that I was some kind of hard-shelled female who had clawed her way up the corporate ladder and now carried a Gucci briefcase and wore only navy pinstriped suits. Female business associates under thirty wanted to invite me to consciousness-raising groups, affirmative action meetings, and bra-burning parties. Older females presumed that I was hiding a Miss. Older males refused to call me anything and usually managed to make at least one derogatory remark about Ms. in the conversation.

In the end, I decided that I would answer to anything. That gave everyone the option of putting me in their favorite pigeonhole. Those who saw me as Mrs. could call me that. The same went for my Ms. friends, and even those who thought I was a Miss could call me comfortably. Everyone was happy, and as long as I remembered to answer to whatever I was called, all went well.

The other night as I was praying, I realized that Jesus uses the same system for names. Jesus has so many names: Redeemer, Savior, Lamb of God, Wonderful, Shepherd, Messiah. And yet, they are all the same person. We can address Jesus with the name that is most comfortable to us.

When I was a new Christian, I knew Jesus only in a very formal way. I called upon the Lord Jesus Christ. Later, I came to know Jesus as a personal Savior, and I used that form of address. Now, I know Jesus as a friend as well, and I use "Dear Jesus" in my prayers. That is the reality of Jesus. And whenever we call him, by whatever name, Jesus hears us and answers.

P.S. The other day, I got my usual allotment of junk mail. There were four letters, identical except for one small detail. They were addressed to Mrs., Ms., Miss, and Mr. Wilson. I think I would have settled for Occupant.

21.

Spices and Cucumbers

Blow upon my garden, that
the spices thereof may flow out.,

—Song of Solomon 4:16

It was the regular Wednesday night Bible study, and I was feeling rather peeved. The minister who usually led the study had been called away. The substitute for the evening had been announced in the Sunday bulletin, but since I had never heard of him, I didn't see any reason to give this Wednesday evening a miss.

This is so often the case in church. Just when I get settled in a comfortable routine, knowing just which way the service is going to go and just how the minister is going to preach and just what kind of music to expect, someone changes something. Either the organist wants to introduce a new tune to my favorite hymn, or the preacher decides to try a "dialogue" sermon, or the elders think that the offertory should come after the pastoral prayer and not before. It's very unsettling.

That's why I had come to depend on Wednesday nights. They were always the same. They followed a set pattern, and I could count on at least one new insight into the particular passage we were studying. I knew the theological stand of the minister and what kind of response he expected from us. It was all very comfortable.

From the moment our pinch hitter opened his mouth, I knew I was in trouble. He had a very thick Scottish accent, nearly unintelligible to me. Since most of the people who regularly attended the Bible study were Scots, they loved him. In fact, with a little encouragement, he would lapse into Gaelic and lose me altogether.

We had been studying First Corinthians, but this fellow decided that we should make a slight side trip into the Song of Solomon instead. Now, I know very little about the Song of Solomon. In fact, it took me a little while to find it.

It became abundantly clear that he had every intention of either skipping over or ignoring completely the "juicy" parts, and in order to keep everything very decent and in good order, he chose to use the King James Version of the Bible. That's the one with all the "thees" and "thous" and "spakes" and "smotes."

Somewhere around the third chapter, I opted out. With the ease of long practice, I arranged my face into an interested expression, settled back, and let my thoughts roam. The rich accents of our leader provided a nice backdrop as I planned the next week's menus, what I would wear to work tomorrow, and how I was going to budget for a new coat.

Eventually, I ran out of plans. In order to forestall my growing boredom, I started to peruse the Song of Solomon open before me. Once I got started, I found it had a kind of rhythm and beauty that made it enjoyable to read.

A verse in chapter four really caught my attention because of the picture it conjured up in my mind: "Awake, O north wind; and come, thou south; blow upon my garden, that the spices thereof may flow out." A few verses earlier, the garden had been described as having "spikenard and saffron; calamus and cinnamon, with all trees of frankincense; myrrh and aloes, with all the chief spices."

I could easily imagine the wonderful smell of the mixed spices wafting out upon the evening air as the wind blew across the garden. My imagination led me further, and I could see that Christians were like spice gardens, waiting for the winds of the Spirit to blow across them and waft their sweet perfumes to the waiting world around. I liked the idea. What a lovely garden I must be!

I finished the Song of Solomon, but the leader still droned on, reciting snatches of Robbie Burns poetry and telling esoteric Scottish legends. So I continued into the next book, which happens to be Isaiah. I had read some of the more well-known prophecies in Isaiah, but the first chapter was completely new to me. Verse eight jumped out at me. "And the daughter of Zion is left as a cottage in a vineyard, as a lodge in a garden of cucumbers, as a besieged city."

"A garden of cucumbers"! My ever-vivid imagination brought forth a picture of cucumbers—nasty, prickly things, hidden under hairy vines, overgrown and pungent, disaster for the indigestion-prone, and apt to prove bitter on the tongue. It was a far cry from the spice garden only three chapters earlier.

I'd rather be a spice garden, but I had a sinking feeling that the cucumber garden is a more accurate description of my life. I'm definitely prickly, and I like it that way—it's better than erecting a "no trespassing" sign, and it has the same effect. My life is covered with vines—vines tying me to the material things of this world that I think I need for my security.

I certainly was capable of causing more than one case of spiritual indigestion with my zealous "holier-than-thou" attitude which I could adopt at the drop of a platitude. As for proving bitter—that was the hardest similarity to admit. It's so much easier to be bitter and blame everyone else than it is to be forgiving and blame no one.

A garden of cucumbers. The description fitted. I wished I had never come to the Bible study in the first place. This was just the kind of insight I didn't need.

Then I remembered the verse in the Song of Solomon. It was the wind blowing across the garden that caused the perfumes to be wafted out. I suddenly realized that the wind of the Holy Spirit could just as easily blow across a garden of cucumbers. But what would waft out? Not the smell of cucumbers, but the sweet odor of the Holy Spirit: the frankincense of prayer, the myrrh of faith, the sweet spice of hope. Where I could only see cucumbers, the Lord had a spice garden. All it needed was the power of the Holy Spirit to release it.

What a wonderful idea! My cucumber garden could produce the fruits of the Spirit simply by asking the Holy Spirit to blow upon my garden—my cucumber garden!

P.S. I didn't find out much about the Song of Solomon that Wednesday night, but I did receive a whole new insight into my life as a Christian.